IMAGES
of America

WEST CHESTER PIKE

The only form of public transportation along the West Chester Road during most of the 1800s was stagecoach. This advertisement from 1887 is for the Newtown & Philadelphia Stage Coach, which was operated by William Snite. It ran from Newtown Square to the William Penn Hotel at Thirty-eighth and Market Streets in Philadelphia, leaving in the mornings and returning in the evenings. Round-trips were offered daily. Passengers had to transfer to horse cars at Thirty-eighth and Market Streets to reach downtown Philadelphia. Single-fare prices for the four stops along the route—Newtown Square, Broomall, Manoa, and Upper Darby—were 50¢, 40¢, 30¢, and 10¢, respectively. Discounted round-trip fares made the same day were 75¢, 60¢, and 45¢ for stops west of Upper Darby. The journey took a little more than two hours each way. (Upper Darby Historical Society, Pennsylvania.)

ON THE COVER: This February 1952 photograph by David H. Cope looks westward on West Chester Pike at Country Club Lane, just east of Manoa Road in Haverford Township. A Philadelphia Suburban Transportation Company trolley is traveling east toward Sixty-ninth Street Terminal in Upper Darby as it passes Suburban Dairies, where Mrs. Joseph Gormley (Mary) was the proprietor. Today, an office building stands where the dairy business once was. A Dunkin' Donuts store is on the open lot across the street at the intersection with Shelbourne Road. (Greco family.)

IMAGES
of America

WEST CHESTER PIKE

Stephen J. Edgcumbe

ARCADIA
PUBLISHING

Copyright © 2012 by Stephen J. Edgcumbe
ISBN 978-0-7385-9244-2

Published by Arcadia Publishing
Charleston, South Carolina

Printed in the United States of America

Library of Congress Control Number: 2011944189

For all general information, please contact Arcadia Publishing:
Telephone 843-853-2070
Fax 843-853-0044
E-mail sales@arcadiapublishing.com
For customer service and orders:
Toll-Free 1-888-313-2665

Visit us on the Internet at www.arcadiapublishing.com

*This book is dedicated to my father, Clifford D. Edgcumbe Sr.,
who instilled in me an interest in and appreciation for history.*

Contents

ACKNOWLEDGMENTS

A variety of sources assisted in the compilation of this photographic history of West Chester Pike, including many individuals, local historical societies and municipalities, a historical museum, and a number of local businesses. Some offered access to their collections of historic photographs, books, magazines, and newspaper clippings. Others simply offered their time to tell their stories. Every effort has been made to identify original sources for photographs. In many cases, original sources could not be identified. I would like to thank Abby Henry, Erin Vosgien, and everyone at Arcadia Publishing for their perseverance and patience in seeing this project through from inception to completion.

I would also like to thank the following: Pamela C. Powell, photograph archivist at the Chester County Historical Society in West Chester, Pennsylvania, for access to its Gilbert Cope Collection of photographs and other resources; Margaret F. Johnson, archivist at the Delaware County Historical Society in Chester, Pennsylvania; Judy Stevenson and John Williams, archivists at the Hagley Museum and Library in Wilmington, Delaware, for access to its Red Arrow Collection of photographs and library resources; Barbara Marinelli and Beverly Rorer of the Upper Darby Historical Society, Pennsylvania; Mary Courtney and Carolyn Joseph of the Haverford Township Historical Society, Pennsylvania; Christopher Driscoll of the Newtown Square Historical Preservation Society, Pennsylvania; the Greco family, owners of the Thunderbird Restaurant in Broomall, Pennsylvania; Seth Pancoast Jr.; Rick Smith, township manager of East Goshen Township, Pennsylvania; Eric Hartline, friend and photographer; Eugene F. Blaum of the Pennsylvania Department of Transportation; Dan Miller, retired Pennsylvania Department of Transportation engineer; Delaware County historians and authors Thomas J. DiFilippo and Thomas R. Smith; Chester County historian and author Bruce Mowday; local historians and collectors Stanley F. Bowman Jr., Keith Lockhart, and Robert Quay; SS. Simon and Jude Catholic Church in West Chester, Pennsylvania; Frank Pica, owner of Pica's Restaurant in Upper Darby, Pennsylvania; Phil Heron, editor of the *Delaware County Daily Times* in Primos, Pennsylvania; John McLaughlin, owner of McLaughlin's Automotive Service Center in West Chester, Pennsylvania; Pegasus Print and Copy Center in Broomall, Pennsylvania; and Steve Allen of Jacob Low Hardware in Havertown, Pennsylvania.

INTRODUCTION

Thank you for picking up *West Chester Pike*. Through photographs and words, this book tells the story of a 20-mile stretch of roadway in southeastern Pennsylvania that connects the city of Philadelphia with the borough of West Chester. The story is told in broad strokes and is intended for a general audience. Other resources on this topic are listed on the bibliography page.

Today, West Chester Pike is a busy, four-lane state highway that is a part of Pennsylvania Route 3. Route 3 runs east-west through Philadelphia along various one-way roads. At Sixty-third Street, also known as Cobbs Creek Parkway, at the western edge of the city, Route 3 becomes Market Street and continues west into Delaware County and the municipalities of Millbourne and Upper Darby. The route remains Market Street for about one mile. It becomes West Chester Pike after rounding the corner past the Sixty-ninth Street Terminal building at Garrett Road in Upper Darby. It continues west through Upper Darby and into Haverford, Marple, Newtown, and Edgmont Townships. In Delaware County, West Chester Pike intersects US Route 1 (Township Line Road) at the border of Upper Darby and Haverford Townships, Interstate 476 near the border of Haverford and Marple Townships, Pennsylvania Route 320 (Sproul Road) in Marple Township, and Pennsylvania Route 252 (Newtown Street Road) in Newtown Township.

After Edgmont Township, the route crosses into Chester County and Willistown, Westtown, East Goshen, and West Goshen Townships. It intersects Pennsylvania Route 926 (Street Road) in Willistown, Pennsylvania Route 352 (Chester Road) in Westtown, and US Routes 202 and 322 (the West Chester Bypass) in West Goshen. Near West Chester, Route 3/West Chester Pike ends and merges with Paoli Pike. It continues one-way west as Gay Street and moves into the borough of West Chester. Route 3/West Chester Pike departs West Chester eastbound by Market Street. After West Chester, the route splits into Pennsylvania Route 162 and US Route 322. Route 322 continues as Downingtown Pike, while Route 162 continues as Strasburg Road. Both roads meander westward through Chester County, changing names and route numbers while moving toward Lancaster County.

It is easy to forget, however, that modern-day West Chester Pike cuts through a former wilderness area once inhabited by the Lenni Lenape, or Delaware Indians, prior to the arrival of Swedish, Dutch, and English settlers in the 1600s. The only "roads" prior to this, most likely, were Indian trails. The area began to change in 1681, when King Charles II of England settled a debt with the family of William Penn by signing the Charter of Pennsylvania, which granted Penn the territory of Pennsylvania. Originally called "Sylvania," meaning "forest land," it was renamed Pennsylvania, meaning "Penn's Forest" or "Penn's Woods," after William Penn's father, Adm. Sir William Penn. William Penn, an English Quaker, began selling land grants to other Quaker settlers.

In 1682, Penn established Chester County, which included present-day Delaware and Lancaster Counties. The county seat of Chester County was set in Chester on the Delaware River. Lancaster County was not established until 1729. Delaware County came along in 1789.

In 1699, Penn called for a road to connect a proposed inland town in modern-day Newtown Township—"Central Square" or "New Town"—with Philadelphia. Penn's dream town, however, was never realized. Meanwhile, roads during this early colonial period served mainly to connect Quakers with the various "Friends," or Quaker meetinghouses, in the area.

In 1754, a road was laid out from Cobbs Creek to Darby Road in Haverford Township. Colonial settlers moved into areas west of Philadelphia by this route as well as by other routes.

Transportation along what was to become the West Chester Road developed slowly over the years. Between 1793 and 1850, the route was a dirt road used by horse-drawn carriages and wagons. In early 1848, however, farmers and mill owners called for state legislation to create a better road on which to move products to market. At certain times of the year, such as after heavy rainfall, sections of the road were impassable. Their efforts for legislation proved successful.

The Philadelphia and West Chester Turnpike Road Company was organized in March 1848 to build a toll road, or turnpike, from the William Penn Hotel at Thirty-eighth and Market Streets in Philadelphia to Newtown Square, about half the distance to West Chester. The road was one of several built in Delaware County in the 1840s to improve farming and manufacturing businesses in the county. Five tollhouses with gates on "pikes" were set up along the route to finance road construction and maintenance. Passage was gained by paying the toll and having the toll keeper "turn the pike." The legislation also authorized townships through which the road passed to purchase stock.

Between 1850 and 1868, the route became a plank road. Wooden planks—first hemlock, and then oak—were used to pave the road. By 1868, stone began to be used to pave sections of the roadway. By 1885, stone was used all the way to Newtown Square, but the road remained dirt between Newtown Square and West Chester.

In 1859, the turnpike company established a horse-drawn railcar service along a four-mile stretch from the William Penn Hotel at Thirty-eighth and Market Streets to the Howard House, an inn at West Chester Pike and Pennock Avenue in Upper Darby. In 1895, the Philadelphia and West Chester Traction Company opened a trolley line from Sixty-third Street to Newtown Square using steam dummies. In 1896, electric trolley car service to Newtown Square began. By late 1898, trolley car service to West Chester was completed. Trolley service to Ardmore via West Chester Pike and Darby Road in Haverford Township was added in 1902.

In 1907, the Sixty-ninth Street Terminal, a transportation hub connecting Philadelphia with emerging western communities, was built in Upper Darby. These events along West Chester Pike brought increasing development to communities west of the city, gradually changing the landscape from rural to suburban. In 1918, the route became a state highway. The tolls were removed, and the turnpike company went out of existence.

A trolley line ran up and down the south side of West Chester Pike between 1898 and 1954. The West Chester trolley line ceased regular operations in June 1954 as plans to widen the roadway commenced. Trolley cars were replaced by buses. Limited trolley service continued along the route during peak travel hours until 1958. Trolley service to Ardmore via West Chester Pike stopped at the end of 1966. The late 1950s and 1960s saw the length of West Chester Pike widened from two to four lanes. In the process, homeowners and businesses were displaced.

West Chester Pike takes readers on an east-west journey that passes through place names familiar to locals, such as the Highland Park and Kirklyn sections of Upper Darby, the Llanerch and Manoa sections of Haverford, the Brookthorpe Hills and Broomall sections of Marple, the Larchmont, St. Albans, and Newtown Square sections of Newtown, the Castle Rock section of Edgmont, the Plumsock and Willistown Knoll sections of Willistown, the Goshen Heights and Milltown sections of East Goshen, and the Chatwood section of West Goshen.

Photographs of historic homes, hotels, inns, and taverns that dotted the route also are featured. Some are gone, such as the Red Lion Inn and the Howard House in Upper Darby; the Eagle Hotel in Haverford; the Drove Tavern in Marple; and the Newtown Square Hotel in Newtown. Some, however, remain, and many have found new uses, such as the Fox Chase Inn in Newtown; the Old President Inn and Tavern in Edgmont; the Willistown Inn and the William Penn Hotel in Willistown; and the Sheaf of Wheat Inn in East Goshen.

Enjoy the ride!

One

MILLBOURNE BOROUGH

Samuel Sellers, who immigrated to America in 1682 from Derbyshire, England, first occupied Millbourne Borough. Sellers, a Quaker, purchased land here from William Penn in 1690. In 1757, the Sellers family started a mill operation along Cobbs Creek, near present-day Sixty-third and Market Streets in Philadelphia. The Lenni Lenape, or Delaware Indians, called Cobbs Creek "Karakung." It was named after William Cobb, who bought the Old Swedes Mill along the creek in Darby Borough from a Swedish company. The Sellers family was among several prominent and influential families who contributed greatly to the growth and development of present-day Millbourne and Upper Darby in the 18th and 19th centuries. Their mill operations in Millbourne grew and flourished into the 1920s. Millbourne was separated from Upper Darby Township and incorporated as a borough in 1909.

The tiny borough of Millbourne runs along the north side of Route 3/Market Street for about one mile, from Sixty-third Street to Chatham Road. Upper Darby runs along the south side of this corridor. After the Sixty-ninth Street Terminal building, Market Street becomes West Chester Pike. (Eric Hartline.)

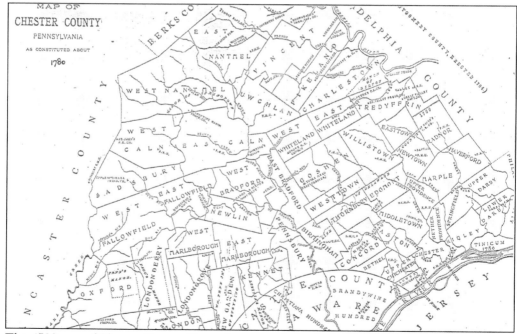

This 1780 map of Chester County, Pennsylvania, includes the land that is now Delaware County. Chester County originally included present-day Lancaster and Delaware Counties. Lancaster County was established in 1729. Delaware County was established in 1789. (Delaware County Historical Society, Pennsylvania.)

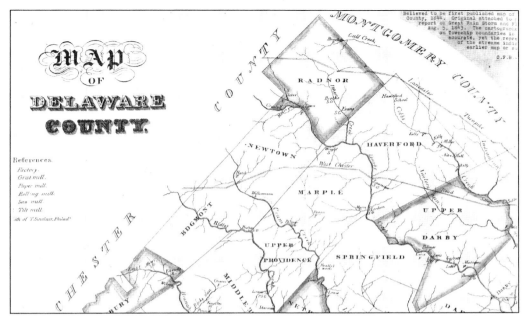

This c. 1844 map of Delaware County shows the West Chester Road moving through Upper Darby, Haverford, Marple, Newtown, and Edgmont. It also references the mills along the route at Cobbs Creek, Darby Creek, Crum Creek, and Ridley Creek. The county seat of Delaware County was originally established in Chester. In 1851, it was moved to Media. (Delaware County Historical Society, Pennsylvania.)

Shown here is the John Sellers Gristmill on Cobbs Creek just west of Sixty-third and Market Streets in Philadelphia. John Sellers's grandfather Samuel Sellers purchased this land from William Penn in 1690. John Sellers built a flour mill here in 1757. It was one of the earliest mills in the area. It was replaced by this gristmill, which dates to 1814, as indicated on the roof gable stone that reads: "1814, J. Sellers." (Delaware County Historical Society, Pennsylvania.)

This photograph shows the Millbourne Mills site around 1880. At this time, the mill operation had grown into the most productive flour mill in the country. The mill continued to grow and expand over the years, all the way into the 1920s. (Upper Darby Historical Society, Pennsylvania.)

The north face of Millbourne Mills is shown here around 1903. In addition to its mill operations, the company went on to house coal, lumber, and ice businesses. The mill encouraged the building of a railroad spur that brought more business to the area. Across the road on the left are the buildings for Derr Lumber and Kunkel Coal. (Upper Darby Historical Society, Pennsylvania.)

This c. 1900 view of Millbourne Mills looks west along Market Street from Sixty-third Street. Mill operations continued on this site until 1925, when a Sears, Roebuck & Co. store was built there. Sears closed its doors in 1988, but the building remained unoccupied. It was demolished in 2001, and the site is vacant today. (Hagley Museum and Library.)

This 1908 photograph looks east on Market Street toward Sixty-third Street, showing the newly constructed elevated trolley tracks with a trolley headed from Philadelphia toward the Sixty-ninth Street Terminal in Upper Darby. The small building in the center is a tollhouse. Behind the tracks is Millbourne Mills with its tall smoke stack. The train tracks on the right served Derr Lumber and Kunkel Coal, located around the bend near Sixty-third Street. (Upper Darby Historical Society, Pennsylvania.)

This c. 1916 photograph faces west on Market Street as the road bends and heads uphill. A tollhouse is shown on the right. The tollhouses were gone by 1918, when the road became a state road. (Upper Darby Historical Society, Pennsylvania.)

This 1920s westward view is seen from the elevated tracks. On the left are the railroad tracks, which served area industries and businesses. On the far left, two spires from the Burd Orphan Asylum can be seen above the tree line. The asylum opened at Sixty-third and Market Streets in 1863 and remained in operation until 1920. The building was razed in the 1930s. (Upper Darby Historical Society, Pennsylvania.)

This c. 1900 photograph shows a westward view along Market Street from a point just west of present-day Powell Lane. The Sellers Estate, or Millbourne, with its stone wall runs along the north side of the road (right). In the distance, people can be seen walking down the road. (Hagley Museum and Library.)

This c. 1900 photograph looks north from Market Street (west of present-day Powell Lane) and shows the gated entrance to the Sellers Estate, also known as Millbourne. (Hagley Museum and Library.)

Two

Upper Darby Township

Present-day Upper Darby is one of the earliest settlements west of Philadelphia. The Lenni Lenape Indians roamed the area and were followed by Swedish, Dutch, and English settlers in the 1600s. English Quakers had a profound influence on the settlement of the area. Upper Darby was formed out of Darby Township in 1736. The early part of the 1900s saw a population explosion in Upper Darby. By the 1960s, the township was one of the most populated municipalities in Pennsylvania, surpassing several cities.

Route 3 crosses the eastern border of Upper Darby as Market Street near Sixty-third and Market Streets. It changes from Market Street to West Chester Pike at the Garrett Road intersection and continues west to Township Line Road, US Route 1, the border with Haverford Township. (Eric Hartline.)

This c. 1899 photograph looks west on Market Street from a point just east of where the Sixty-ninth Street Terminal would be built in 1907. The construction of the transportation hub changed this rural scene dramatically and forever. Three people stand in the road next to the open field that would soon be replaced by the terminal building, sets of rails, and arriving and departing railcars. (Hagley Museum and Library.)

Facing west from a point on
Market Street just east of 69th
Street Terminal, left—1916, right
—the same spot today.

The inset photograph on the left also looks west on Market Street just east of the Sixty-ninth Street Terminal in 1916. The photograph on the right is the same scene in 1943. (Upper Darby Historical Society, Pennsylvania.)

The Sixty-ninth Street Terminal is shown here around 1916. This view looks east along Market Street. (Upper Darby Historical Society, Pennsylvania.)

The intersection of West Chester Pike and Victory Avenue, going off to the right, is shown here around 1926. Horse-drawn wagons are still being used along with cars and trucks. The building in the center is the train control tower. (Upper Darby Historical Society, Pennsylvania.)

A woman, perhaps the proprietress, can be seen in this c. 1900 photograph standing on the porch of a cigar store at the intersection of West Chester Pike and Garrett Road. Across the street is the Bond Feed Store with a sign advertising Arlington Cemetery. The trolley tracks can be seen running in front of the store. (Upper Darby Historical Society, Pennsylvania.)

The Red Lion Hotel and Tavern was built in 1796. It was a log house covered with boards. It remained a public roadhouse until 1815, when its license was taken away. It is shown here around 1914. It stood on the north side of West Chester Pike about where Leighton Terrace is today. (Upper Darby Historical Society, Pennsylvania.)

This c. 1900 photograph looking eastward from a point near present-day Keystone Avenue shows a barn building at left and the trolley tracks at right. A young girl can be seen in the distance on the left side of the roadway. (Hagley Museum and Library.)

Pictured is a 1942 aerial view of Sixty-ninth Street. By this time, the area was a bustling shopping district and transportation hub. Many of the buildings seen here are still standing today. Market Street/ West Chester Pike runs from left to right near the bottom of the photograph. (Delaware County Historical Society, Pennsylvania.)

An unidentified man stands on the trolley tracks in this c. 1916 photograph, facing east toward Sixty-ninth Street at a point east of State Road. The barn, seen up close in a previous photograph, can be seen at a distance on the left. Two horse-drawn carriages can also be seen making their way west on West Chester Pike. (Upper Darby Historical Society, Pennsylvania.)

This photograph from the 1920s looks east on West Chester Pike near Leighton Terrace toward the Keystone School building, which was built in 1923. A trolley can be seen in front of the building, and a motorcar is driving near a person walking in the road. Today, the Keystone School building serves as the Upper Darby Township Public Safety Building and is home to the police department, a records office, and a courtroom. The original Keystone School building was built in 1875 and still stands next to the public safety building. (Upper Darby Historical Society, Pennsylvania.)

This c. 1916 photograph looks west on West Chester Pike toward Toll Gate No. 2 at State Road. The roof of Wayside, the home of John Sellers (1762–1847), is on the left. A gas lamp is pictured on the right. At the time of this photograph, the grade of the road was higher than the surroundings. It was regraded before it was paved. (Upper Darby Historical Society, Pennsylvania.)

Toll Gate No. 2 at State Road is shown up close in this c. 1916 photograph. The trolley tracks can be seen in the foreground. In many cases, the toll keeper and his family lived in these larger tollgate houses. The gate appears to be open here. The sign out front reads, "Stop, Give Ticket or Pay Toll." (Upper Darby Historical Society, Pennsylvania.)

The Howard House, built in 1810 by Abraham Pennock, was a well-known temperance inn for travelers who opposed the use of alcohol. It stood on the northwest corner of West Chester Pike and Pennock Avenue. Strong evidence indicates that Pennock, a supporter of the abolition movement who helped many slaves to freedom in the mid-1800s, used the Howard House as a stop along the Underground Railroad. It also served as a stagecoach stop, post office, and florist shop. It was remodeled into apartments in 1916. It was demolished in 1973 and made into a parking lot for Pica's Restaurant. (Upper Darby Historical Society, Pennsylvania.)

In 1941, Frank Pica Sr. opened a pizzeria at Sixty-second and Race Streets in West Philadelphia. The business moved to its current location on West Chester Pike and Pennock Avenue in Upper Darby in 1956, where it became a full-service restaurant. This 1960s photograph shows the tracks for the West Chester and Ardmore trolley lines. The tracks were eventually taken up, and a grass median strip was created. (Frank Pica.)

Mary Jones, the daughter of Richard and Sophie Jones, is pictured in 1890 standing on a farm access path near present-day Carol Boulevard and West Chester Pike in the Highland Park section of the township. Mary Jones is facing north. The path behind her leads to West Chester Pike. (Upper Darby Historical Society, Pennsylvania.)

This 1948 photograph presents a westward view along West Chester Pike at Carol Boulevard in the Highland Park section of the township. (Upper Darby Historical Society, Pennsylvania.)

The University of Pennsylvania Flower Observatory property on the north side of West Chester Pike between Carol Boulevard and Cedar Lane is seen in this c. 1900 photograph. The observatory was dismantled in the early 1930s due to light pollution caused by increasing development in Upper Darby. Quality night observations were no longer possible. (Hagley Museum and Library.)

Views on Phila. & West Chester Trolley.   The Flower Observatory. (University of Penna.) Llanerch, Pa.

Here is another view of the Flower Observatory around 1916. Along the north side of this section of West Chester Pike today, there are a number of commercial establishments and apartments. A playground and ball field behind this commercial and residential strip, however, is called the Observatory Hills Recreation Area, a reminder of its past. (Upper Darby Historical Society, Pennsylvania.)

This c. 1910 photograph shows an eastbound view of West Chester Pike at Cedar Lane. A trolley stop is on the right. Two horse-drawn carriages can also be seen traveling west. (Upper Darby Historical Society, Pennsylvania.)

Here is a similar westbound view of West Chester Pike at Cedar Lane around 1920. Several people can be seen waiting at the trolley stop, while a man stands in the middle of the road near a parked car. (Upper Darby Historical Society, Pennsylvania.)

30

This 1941 aerial photograph shows the intersection of West Chester Pike and Township Line Road, the border of Upper Darby and Haverford Townships. It presents an eastbound view of West Chester Pike, which runs from the bottom of the photograph to the top. Township Line Road runs from south to north and right to left. (Delaware County Historical Society, Pennsylvania.)

The corner of West Chester Pike and Linden Avenue in the Kirklyn section of the township was the location of Penman's house furnishings store from 1924 to 1937. Owner Charles Penman is pictured here in 1927. Two gas pumps selling Gulf gasoline and a black oil pump are also pictured. This site was also the home of the Kirklyn Pharmacy for many years. A clothes-cleaning business operates at the site today. (Upper Darby Historical Society, Pennsylvania.)

In this c. 1916 photograph, a horse-drawn wagon makes its way east on West Chester Pike just below Township Line Road in the Kirklyn section of the township. Kirklyn was named after the Kirk family, prominent landowners in Upper Darby since 1688. (Upper Darby Historical Society, Pennsylvania.)

Three

HAVERFORD TOWNSHIP

Haverford Township was founded by Welsh Quakers in 1681 from land purchased by William Penn. It is named for Haverford-West in Pembrokeshire, South Wales. The township was primarily agricultural until the early part of the 1900s, when road and transportation improvements brought many new residents to the area and with them a demand for new housing. As a result, many suburban communities were built in the township.

West Chester Pike crosses the eastern border of the township at Township Line Road (US Route 1). To the west, it departs the township at Darby Creek near the intersection with Lawrence Road and enters Marple Township. (Eric Hartline.)

This late-1920s photograph looks eastward on West Chester Pike toward the intersection of Township Line Road (US Route 1) in the Llanerch section of Haverford Township. The trolley car shown is bound for Ardmore. It will soon turn right and travel north along Darby Road to reach its destination. (Stanley F. Bowman Jr.)

This c. 1900 photograph looks east along West Chester Pike from a point just east of Darby Road. (Hagley Museum and Library.)

This postcard shows the original building, which housed a drugstore and later a grocery store, on the north side of West Chester Pike at Darby Road in the Llanerch section. The building, which has been expanded and remodeled, stands today and houses the Llanerch Fire Company. (Keith Lockhart.)

The intersection of West Chester Pike and Darby Road is pictured here around the 1940s. West Chester Pike, looking west, is straight ahead. Darby Road veers off to the right. (Haverford Township Historical Society, Havertown, Pennsylvania.)

Here is another view of the intersection at West Chester Pike and Darby Road from February 1966. Darby Road is in the foreground. West Chester Pike, looking west, is to the far left. The office building pictured here is now gone. On this corner today is the Llanerch Crossing Park. (Haverford Township Historical Society, Havertown, Pennsylvania.)

The wall mural at Llanerch Crossing Park at West Chester Pike and Darby Road is seen in a 2011 photograph. The park was created at the intersection in 2006. The mural depicts the Battle of Llanerch Crossing, an 1895 legal battle over rail crossing rights between the Philadelphia and West Chester Traction Company and the Pennsylvania Railroad. The traction company was building a trolley line connecting Philadelphia with West Chester, and the railroad was building a train line from Philadelphia to Newtown Square. The two lines crossed at a point just west of the intersection. In July 1895, while the battle over crossing rights was being fought in court, trolley and railroad construction crews confronted each other at Llanerch. Words were exchanged, a few fights broke out, and shootings were threatened. A few arrests were made, but further violence was averted. Eventually, the crossing was laid. (Eric Hartline.)

A Philadelphia Suburban Transportation Co. maintenance car is pictured in 1949 parked outside the Llanerch Power House at the intersection of West Chester Pike and Darby Road. This car was built by the Jewett Car Co. as a freight car in 1911. It still goes out fixing overhead wires for the Southeastern Pennsylvania Transportation Authority (SEPTA) to this day. (Bob Quay Sr.)

Kohl's Department Store now occupies the site of the old Red Arrow bus barn (near West Chester Pike and Darby Road), pictured here in 1948. The tracks in the foreground are those of the Pennsylvania Railroad Newtown Square Branch. (Bob Quay Sr.)

This c. 1900 photograph shows a Philadelphia and West Chester Traction Company double-track open trolley car. (Hagley Museum and Library.)

This c. 1910 postcard looks north from West Chester Pike across Darby Road and toward Park Road in the Llanerch section of the township. Two well-dressed women can be seen walking down Park Road past a house in this new suburban area. The tracks seen in the postcard are for the Ardmore trolley line, which ran along Darby Road. (Keith Lockhart.)

This c. 1900 photograph looks west along West Chester Pike from a point just east of the Philadelphia and West Chester Traction Company office. It also shows the Pennsylvania Railroad and trolley line crossing, which is about 100 yards west of the West Chester Pike and Darby Road intersection. A Burger King restaurant and a public storage facility are at this approximate site today. (Hagley Museum and Library.)

This c. 1900 photograph looks west along West Chester Pike from a point just east of Manoa Road. (Hagley Museum and Library.)

This c. 1900 photograph is in the same location as the previous photograph, but it looks east along West Chester Pike from a point near Country Club Lane, which is just east of Manoa Road. A Dunkin' Donuts store is at this approximate location today. (Hagley Museum and Library.)

Here are two views of Samuel Moore's general store and post office, which stood on the northeast corner of West Chester Pike and Manoa Road, where a law office is located today. The image above is undated and looks north along Manoa Road from West Chester Pike. The image below, from the Hilda Lucas Collection, is from 1894. Samuel Moore is pictured in white shirt sleeves with his hands on his hips. (Both, Haverford Township Historical Society, Havertown, Pennsylvania.)

This is an interior shot of Samuel Moore's general store and post office in the Manoa section of the township. The photograph is undated, and the man behind the counter is not identified. (Upper Darby Historical Society, Pennsylvania.)

This c. 1900 photograph looks south along a rural Manoa Road at its intersection with West Chester Pike. Today, the Manoa Medical Center is where this house and small barn once stood. The fence to the left runs along the present-day Llanerch Country Club property. (Hagley Museum and Library.)

This c. 1900 photograph looks west along West Chester Pike from Manoa Road. (Hagley Museum and Library.)

The building seen here stands on the north side of West Chester Pike near the intersection of Washington Avenue, just east of Eagle Road. In this c. 1950s photograph, it appears the building was home to many groups and enterprises. It served as an Independent Order of Odd Fellows lodge, a Masonic lodge, a Baptist church, a post office, and an insurance company office. It is presently used for commercial purposes. (Keith Lockhart.)

The Eagle Hotel, established in 1814 on the northeast corner of West Chester Pike and Eagle Road, is seen in this c. 1900 photograph. It was a popular stopping place for road-weary travelers. A row of stores stands on this corner today. (Hagley Museum and Library.)

Here is another view of the Eagle Hotel from 1907. A horse carriage is parked outside, and several men can be seen sitting on the porch behind the horses. Eagle Road is on the left. The trolley tracks along West Chester Pike are seen in the far right corner. (Keith Lockhart.)

This February 1966 photograph shows the row of stores on the northeast corner of Eagle Road and West Chester Pike, including the DiBona Pharmacy and the Jacob Low Hardware Store, which today stands about 100 feet east of its location here. (Haverford Township Historical Society, Havertown, Pennsylvania.)

The south side of West Chester Pike near Eagle Road is shown in this February 1952 photograph by Bob Fox. Pictured are the Manoa Inn and Club Del Rio. For many years, this site was home to L&M Caterers. Today, the building is called the L&M Professional Building and houses a number of businesses. (Haverford Township Historical Society, Havertown, Pennsylvania.)

The Eagle Road Pharmacy, on the southeast corner of West Chester Pike and Eagle Road, is shown in this February 1966 photograph. A parking lot and a Starbucks Coffee store stand at this site today. (Haverford Township Historical Society, Havertown, Pennsylvania.)

In this David H. Cope photograph from February 1952, a trolley car is shown traveling west on West Chester Pike just past the Eagle Road intersection. A trolley stop can be seen near the southwest corner of the intersection. Across the street, gasoline is selling for 18¢ a gallon. (Jacob Low Hardware.)

This c. 1900 photograph looks west along West Chester Pike toward the fourth tollhouse at Manoa, or Westgate Hills, just west of the present-day Manoa Shopping Center. (Hagley Museum and Library.)

This 1950s photograph shows a westward view at the entrance to Old West Chester Pike near Darby Creek and Lawrence Road. An eastbound trolley is climbing the hill. The railing for the bridge over the creek is to the left of the tracks, near the cars. Today, a Barnaby's of America restaurant sits down and to the left of the road. (Haverford Township Historical Society, Havertown, Pennsylvania.)

The Adele Post Office, which stood on the south side of Old West Chester Pike near Lawrence Road, is shown in this c. 1900 photograph. The trolley track can be seen running past the building. It was near the old Smith's Saw Mill property and the Lawrence Cabin. (Hagley Museum and Library.)

This 1941 photograph shows Smith's Saw Mill, which was located on Old West Chester Pike at Lawrence Road next to Darby Creek. A mill operated continuously at this site from the 1700s until the 1980s. The first owner, Humphrey Ellis, operated a wool-processing mill at the site. In 1807, the Lawrence family ran a gristmill here. In the 1930s, Robert H. Smith converted the operation into a sawmill. The sawmill operated until 1987. (Haverford Township Historical Society, Havertown, Pennsylvania.)

The Lawrence Cabin, or Three Generation House, is shown here at its original location near the banks of the Darby Creek on Old West Chester Pike. It was located near present-day West Chester Pike and Lawrence Road, which is now the site of a carwash business and restaurant. The center section of the cabin dates to 1710, and the two outside sections were later additions. In the early 1960s, the cabin was scheduled for demolition. The Haverford Township Historical Society, however, stepped in to save this piece of history. The structure was carefully dismantled, moved, and rebuilt on Karakung Drive in Powder Mill Valley Park as part of the township's Colonial Living Program. It sits next to another historic landmark, Nitre Hall. (Chester County Historical Society, West Chester, Pennsylvania.)

This c. 1900 photograph looks west along Old West Chester Pike from a point just east of the Darby Creek Bridge, where people can be seen standing on the right. In the distance is the beginning of Marple Township. (Hagley Museum and Library.)

This 2011 photograph looks west along West Chester Pike toward the Darby Creek Bridge and Lawrence Road at the border of Haverford and Marple Townships. The 21.5-mile Mid-County Expressway, or Veterans Memorial Highway, intersects the road here. Known locally as the Blue Route, it runs north-south through Delaware County and Montgomery County, connecting Interstate 95 near Chester with the Pennsylvania Turnpike (Interstate 276) and the Northeast Turnpike Extension in Plymouth Township, Montgomery County. It is part of a 132-mile auxiliary state highway, Interstate 476, which runs between Interstate 95 and Interstate 81 north of Scranton, Pennsylvania. This 21.5-mile portion of the highway opened to traffic in December 1991 after more than six decades of planning, controversy, and on-and-off construction. (Eric Hartline.)

This 1949 photograph looks east on West Chester Pike, just west of the Darby Creek Bridge at Lawrence Road near the border of Haverford and Marple Townships. A westbound trolley is traveling through the snow past a roadside hamburger restaurant called Tim's (left). (Haverford Township Historical Society, Havertown, Pennsylvania.)

Here is a similar view from 1951 looking east on West Chester Pike, just west of the Darby Creek Bridge at Lawrence Road near Tim's Restaurant. This photograph was taken during more mild weather. (Haverford Township Historical Society, Havertown, Pennsylvania.)

Four

MARPLE TOWNSHIP

English Quakers established Marple Township in 1684. Early landowners in Marple were Francis Stanfield, Jonathon Hayes, and John Howell. Stanfield, whose daughter was born in Marpool, England, may have been responsible for naming the township. Over the course of the last 300 years, Marple has evolved from a small, rural farming community to a thriving and diverse suburban community of approximately 25,000 residents.

West Chester Pike crosses the eastern border of Marple Township at Darby Creek near the intersection with Lawrence Road. It continues west until it reaches Media Line Road, which is the border with Newtown Township. (Eric Hartline.)

The Bergdoll Mansion stood on the north side of West Chester Pike near the present-day Interstate 476, or Blue Route, interchange. The impressive home was built around 1900. It is seen in this 1940s photograph. The resident of the house was the wealthy Grover Cleveland Bergdoll, an early aviator, race car driver, and World War I draft dodger who went to Germany to avoid military service. The mansion burned down in the mid-1970s. (Greco family.)

This c. 1900 photograph looks east along West Chester Pike from a point just west of Darby Creek and Lawrence Road and from Marple Township toward Haverford Township. This is Old West Chester Pike, which—from this vantage point—runs about 100 yards south of the present-day roadway. (Hagley Museum and Library.)

This 2011 photograph also looks east on West Chester Pike from a point just west of Darby Creek and Lawrence Road at the Blue Route interchange from Marple toward Haverford. It is a similar vantage point as the previous image. As mentioned, the roadway did not originally run in this direction. Old West Chester Pike would have taken the south ramp for Chester here and run about 100 yards before straightening out, crossing Darby Creek, and bending north again. (Eric Hartline.)

The Brookthorpe property, pictured in 2012, sits on the north side of the road at the intersection with New Ardmore Avenue. It is a designated historical site in the eponymously named Brookthorpe Hills section of Marple Township. The Federal-style house was built on land originally owned by Robert Taylor. J.M. Moore constructed the original house in 1821, and an addition was made in the late 19th century. Today, the property is used as office space. (Eric Hartline.)

This c. 1900 photograph looks northeast along West Chester Pike from a point just west of present-day New Ardmore Avenue. The property down the road on the left is believed to be the Brookthorpe property. (Hagley Museum and Library.)

Moore's Luncheonette was a popular stop along West Chester Pike in the Broomall section of Marple Township during the 1930s and 1940s. It was located on the site of the present-day Thunderbird Restaurant at 2323 West Chester Pike next to Glenwood Memorial Gardens Cemetery. Pictured in this late 1940s photograph is the owner, Mr. Moore. (Greco family.)

Sam Greco opened the Thunderbird Restaurant on the site of the old Moore's Luncheonette in the spring of 1956. The restaurant remains in the Greco family today and is run by the sons of Bill Greco Sr. It remains a favorite stop for local residents and travelers along West Chester Pike. Seen in front of the business in a late 1950s photograph is Bill Greco Sr., being given the keys to a new car. (Greco family.)

This 1950s photograph shows an old farmhouse that was on the south side of West Chester Pike at Franklin Getz Drive and across from the Thunderbird Restaurant. On this site today is Marple American Legion Post 805. (Delaware County Historical Society, Pennsylvania.)

This early-1950s photograph looks eastward along West Chester Pike from a point just west of the Pine Valley Road intersection. People exiting this westbound trolley are, most likely, returning home after a day at the office or school. (Greco family.)

This 1940s photograph looks north from Sproul Road (Route 320) toward West Chester Pike and the old Drove Tavern, which operated as a luncheonette during this time period. (Delaware County Historical Society, Pennsylvania.)

Pictured here is the old Drove Tavern building, which dated to 1723. It stood on the northeast corner of West Chester Pike and Sproul Road (Route 320) for more than two centuries. In its later years, it served as a corner store under a variety of names. It was demolished along with the building next to it in the 1950s to widen the Sproul Road intersection. On this corner today is a gourmet food business, a furniture business, and a pizza shop. (Delaware County Historical Society, Pennsylvania.)

A Howard Johnson's restaurant stood on the south side of West Chester Pike near the intersection with Sproul Road in the 1940s. The Country Squire Diner and Restaurant sits near this location today. (Greco family.)

This view from the 1950s looks west along West Chester Pike at the Sproul Road intersection as a parade marches east. (Greco family.)

Here is another view of West Chester Pike and Sproul Road (Route 320) from the 1940s. It looks west along the pike. The Drove Tavern building is on the far right. To the left, on the other side of Sproul Road, is the former Bonsall Brothers General Store and Post Office building. (Delaware County Historical Society, Pennsylvania.)

A parade marches west on West Chester Pike at Sproul Road past the old Drove Tavern in the 1950s. This view looks north from Sproul Road. (Greco family.)

The Bonsall Brothers General Store and Post Office is shown in a photograph from around the 1930s or 1940s with its porch and canopy still intact. It stood on the northwest corner of West Chester Pike and Sproul Road. A popular gathering spot for local residents for many years, it was torn down in the early 1960s, and a gasoline station was built on the site. Today, a McDonald's Restaurant is at this location. (Delaware County Historical Society, Pennsylvania.)

This parade, featuring the Marple-Newtown Junior High School Band, is marching east on West Chester Pike at Sproul Road some time during the 1960s. By this time, the trolly tracks along West Chester Pike had been removed. (Greco family.)

This photograph looks west and presents another view of a 1960s-era parade as it marches east on West Chester Pike at Sproul Road. The Phillips 66 gas station in the background was replaced by a Rustler Steakhouse in the 1970s. The site is now the location of a McDonald's restaurant. (Greco family.)

This eastward view along West Chester Pike at Sproul Road in the Broomall section of Marple Township shows a Philadelphia Suburban Transportation Company trolley heading east toward Upper Darby. At the rear, the trolley is still displaying a sign for the Larchmont stop in Newtown Township. This photograph was taken in March 1954. In the foreground on the right and on the opposite side of Sproul Road is the Howard Johnson's restaurant sign. (David H. Cope.)

This undated photograph shows the Franklin Getz home at 2632 West Chester Pike in the Broomall section of the township. On the south side of the pike, it is now the site of the Marple/Broomall Post Office and an apartment complex. (Delaware County Historical Society, Pennsylvania.)

The Maris House, located just west of Sproul Road (Route 320) at Broomall Avenue, is seen here in 2011. The Maris family came from England in 1682 and settled in nearby Springfield in Delaware County. Family descendants later settled in Marple and built this fieldstone farmhouse on the north side of the roadway around 1800. It remained a private residence until the mid-20th century. It is the former site of Pancoast Gardens and now serves as an animal hospital. (Both, Eric Hartline.)

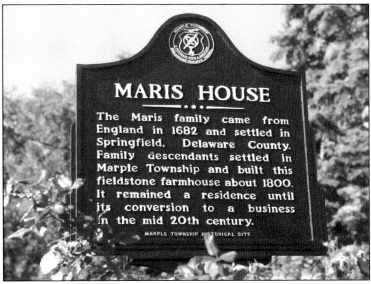

This undated photograph shows the Gardner M. Showalter home, which stood on the south side of the road at 2640 West Chester Pike in the Broomall section of the township. It dated to the mid-1700s. It was eventually torn down and is now the site of a Century 21 Alliance real estate office. (Delaware County Historical Society, Pennsylvania.)

This photograph looks east along West Chester Pike at Malin Road in the 1950s. At left is the old Marple School building, which is no longer there. (Greco family.)

WEST CHESTER PIKE AND MALIN ROAD

The Culbertson House, a fieldstone farmhouse that stands today just west of Malin Road near Harmil Road, was built by noted Quaker Jonathan Maris in 1750. It was purchased by Robert Culbertson after the Civil War and remained in the Culbertson family until the early 20th century. It now houses law offices. (Both, Eric Hartline.)

Toll Gate 5 West Chester Pike, Newtown Square, Pa.

This c. 1910 postcard provides an eastward view along West Chester Pike at Toll House No. 5 between Springfield Road and Media Line Road. This was the first, or last, toll along the original turnpike from Philadelphia to Newtown Square, depending on which way a traveler was going. A Gulf station is at this site today. (Keith Lockhart.)

Five

NEWTOWN TOWNSHIP

Newtown Township dates to 1681 and was incorporated as a township in 1684. William Penn proposed building the first inland town west of Philadelphia at the intersection of Newtown Street Road (Route 252), laid out in 1683, and Goshen Road, laid out in 1687. The town was to be called Central Square or New Town. Penn's dream town, however, never came to fruition. The main intersection of the area later became Newtown Street Road and West Chester Pike. Today, this area is known as Newtown Square.

West Chester Pike crosses the eastern border of Newtown Township at Media Line Road. The road crosses the western border of the township near Crum Creek and Crum Creek Road and enters Edgmont Township. (Eric Hartline.)

Pictured here is a steam dummy car, which was used along West Chester Pike in 1895 when the Philadelphia and West Chester Traction Company opened a trolley line from Sixty-third Street in Philadelphia to Newtown Square. Steam dummies were replaced by electric cars in 1896. This image is from the Hilda Lucas Collection. (Newtown Square Preservation Society.)

This c. 1915 photograph shows West Chester Pike looking west. The exact location is unknown. The uphill view resembles what one would see near Media Line Road in the Valley View Acres or Larchmont sections of the township. (Newtown Square Preservation Society.)

Here is another 1920s or 1930s view of West Chester Pike looking west. Again, the exact location is unknown. The approximate area is in the St. Alban's section of the township. (Newtown Square Preservation Society.)

Today, this building stands on the north side of the roadway just east of Bryn Mawr Avenue. It was alternately known as the Fox Chase Inn and the Fawkes Tavern and dates to 1724. It remained an inn until 1870, when it became a private residence. Today, it houses law offices. (Both, Eric Hartline.)

THE FOX CHASE INN
C. 1724

Called Fawkes Tavern 1727
Renamed The Fox Chase 1814
Operated as Inn until 1870
Delaware County Heritage Award 1993

NEWTOWN SQUARE
HISTORICAL PRESERVATION SOCIETY

The Hood Octagonal School is shown here in a photograph postcard dated 1907. It was one of Newtown's earliest schools. It stands today on the south side of West Chester Pike at School House Lane and Dunwoody Drive, just east of Bryn Mawr Avenue. It is on the grounds of the Dunwoody Village property. (Newtown Square Preservation Society.)

The Hood Octagonal School is seen here in 2011. The eight-sided schoolhouse was built in 1841 and served as a local school for about 25 years before being abandoned. It was restored in the 1960s and was added to the National Register of Historic Places in 2006. (Both, Eric Hartline.)

This c. 1940 photograph of an apparent car accident on West Chester Pike looks west along the roadway. The exact location is not known. The road here resembles the area near the intersection of West Chester Pike and Bryn Mawr Avenue. (Newtown Square Preservation Society.)

This 1940s photograph looks west toward Newtown Street Road (Route 252). The field on the south side of the road to the left of the trolley line is Hanley Farm, the present site of the Newtown Square Shopping Center. (Newtown Square Preservation Society.)

The American Telephone Building, shown here around 1920, stood on the south side of West Chester Pike near Newtown Street Road (Route 252) in the Newtown Square section of the township. (Keith Lockhart.)

This 1920s photograph shows the northwest corner of West Chester Pike and Newtown Street Road. It also shows the Lewis Brothers General Store and a gas station in the building on the far right. To the left are a barbershop and the Newtown Square Hotel. The center building still stands today. A Best Auto Tag store is also at this location. (Newtown Square Preservation Society.)

A late-1940s Memorial Day parade heads east on West Chester Pike in Newtown Square, past the old Acme Market and toward Newtown Street Road (Route 252). The trolley tracks on the south side of the road can be seen in the bottom left corner. The porch of the Newtown Square Hotel can be seen at right. (Newtown Square Preservation Society.)

This c. 1912 postcard shows a panoramic view of the intersection at West Chester Pike and Route 252 (Newtown Street Road) in Newtown Square. The view looks west on West Chester Pike. A trolley car is at left. The Newtown Square Hotel is believed to be behind the trees on the right. (Keith Lockhart.)

Ellis Hall, the main building at the Charles E. Ellis School in Newtown Square, is shown in a c. 1950 postcard. The school was established for fatherless girls in 1919 and closed in the 1970s. It stood on the north side of West Chester Pike on what today is called the Ellis Preserve. It is now the site of offices for SAP America, the Main Line Health Center, and other businesses. (Keith Lockhart.)

This view looks west on West Chester Pike at Boot Road in the late 1940s as a trolley rambles along the track. Today, the building on the right is home to a pizza shop. (Greco family.)

This c. 1915 photograph shows West Chester Pike looking west in Newtown Township near the border with Edgmont Township. The exact location is unknown. A horse carriage can be seen in the distance. (Newtown Square Preservation Society.)

This c. 1900 photograph is looking west on West Chester Pike in the Florida Park section of the township. In the distance are Crum Creek and the Crum Creek Covered Bridge, the outline of which can just be seen. The dirt roadway is full of ruts, which were probably the result of heavy rains. The trolley track is at left. (Newtown Square Preservation Society.)

This c. 1900 photograph looks west along West Chester Pike from a point just east of Crum Creek and the Crum Creek Covered Bridge. The road approaches the section of Castle Rock at the border of Newtown and Edgmont Townships. (Hagley Museum and Library.)

This c. 1900 photograph looks north along Crum Creek from a point south of West Chester Pike and the Crum Creek Covered Bridge. To the right of the creek today is Rafferty Subaru. (Hagley Museum and Library.)

Six

EDGMONT TOWNSHIP

Edgmont was incorporated as a township in 1687. Early documents spell the name "Edgemont," "Edgmond," or "Edgmont," with the township settling on "Edgmont" in the 19th century. The major roads in Edgmont were not paved until the mid-1900s.

West Chester Pike crosses the eastern boundary of Edgmont Township at Crum Creek and Crum Creek Road in the Castle Rock section of the township. The route continues west past Edgmont Country Club and Ridley Creek State Park with Edgmont running along the south side of the road and Willistown Township running along the north side. Edgmont takes its leave of West Chester Pike somewhere around the country club property. (Eric Hartline.)

Views on Phila. & West Chester Trolley.   Old Cotton Mill at Castle Rock. Edgemont, Pa.

This c. 1908 photograph postcard shows the ruins of Hatch's Cotton Mill on the south side of West Chester Pike at Castle Rock in Edgmont Township as seen from the Philadelphia & West Chester Trolley. (Keith Lockhart.)

82

Ridley Creek as seen from the West Chester and Philadelphia Trolley Road.

This c. 1908 postcard photograph shows Ridley Creek along West Chester Pike as seen from the Philadelphia & West Chester Trolley. (Keith Lockhart.)

This undated postcard drawing shows the Castle Rock formations in Edgmont, some of which can still be seen by turning south from West Chester Pike onto Rock Ridge Road. In the late 1800s, Castle Rock was a picturesque, wooded hillside area studded with volcanic rocks more than 100 feet high that were honeycombed with fissures and caverns. Many people were attracted to the natural beauty of the area. Castle Rock was also the site of an amusement park and picnic ground from 1899 to about 1906. It was a popular destination that was easily reached by the new trolley line. (Delaware County Historical Society, Pennsylvania.)

The Old President Inn and Tavern sat on the northeast corner of West Chester Pike and Providence Road. The building dates to the 1700s and is seen in this early-1900s photograph taken by Frederick Shelton. The building remains in use today. Over the years, it has been home to the Edgmont Inn and to Bill Daley's Olde Country Tavern. It is now home to La Locanda Restaurant and Bar. (Chester County Historical Society, West Chester, Pennsylvania.)

Shown is another view of the Old President Inn and Tavern. In this 1952 photograph by Lorraine Carstairs Pierce, an Edgemont Inn sign hangs on the side of the building. The inn used the alternate spelling "Edgemont," as indicated by the sign. On the day of this photograph, clothes were hanging to dry on a line out front. La Locanda Restaurant and Bar operates at the site today. (Chester County Historical Society, West Chester, Pennsylvania.)

An eastbound trolley car stops to pick up and drop off passengers in front of the Edgemont Cash Grocery, which stood on the southwest corner of West Chester Pike and Providence Road. This photograph was taken on June 3, 1954, the last day of regular trolley service to West Chester. A Dairy Queen restaurant stood at this corner for many years. Today, a bank branch office is at the location. (David H. Cope.)

In this eastbound view, a trolley car is shown heading west past the Edgemont Dairy Cottage near the border of Edgmont and Willistown Townships on May 30, 1954. The Dairy Cottage was located on the north side of the road between Plumsock and Delchester Roads. On this approximate site today is the Teikoku Restaurant. Before Teikoku, Bobby's Seafood was at this location. On the right is a farm property. (Bob Quay Sr.)

Seven

WILLISTOWN TOWNSHIP

As West Chester Pike crosses into Willistown Township, it enters Chester County, one of the three original counties created by William Penn in 1682 (the other two being Philadelphia and Bucks Counties). Delaware and Lancaster Counties grew out of Chester County in the 1700s. Willistown Township was established in 1704.

West Chester Pike crosses the eastern border of Willistown Township near Providence Road and Ridley Creek State Park. It crosses the western border of the township near Chester Road (Route 352). (Eric Hartline.)

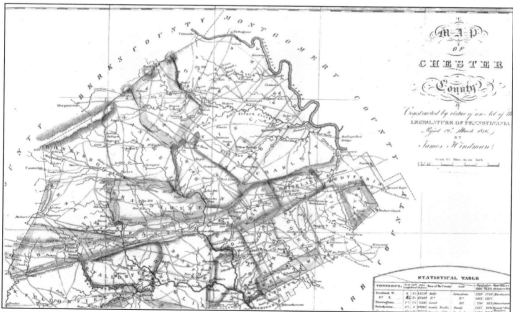

This is a map of Chester County from 1816. (Delaware County Historical Society, Pennsylvania.)

The William Penn Hotel, an R.M. Broomall property, is located on the north side of West Chester Pike, east of Plumsock Road and across from the Edgmont Country Club. It is seen here in a c. 1900 photograph. The building stands today but is unoccupied, and the property is overgrown. (Chester County Historical Society, West Chester, Pennsylvania.)

Here is another view of the William Penn Hotel from 1952. Its appearance has been significantly altered. (Chester County Historical Society, West Chester, Pennsylvania.)

This farmhouse was built by Aaron Garrett in 1802. It stands today on the north side of West Chester Pike and east of Garrett Mill Road. It is shown here in a May 1899 photograph taken by Gilbert Cope. (Chester County Historical Society, West Chester, Pennsylvania.)

This eastward view along West Chester Pike near Garrett Mill Road shows the Ridley Creek Bridge and the Garrett Farm property around 1900. (Chester County Historical Society, West Chester, Pennsylvania.)

Here is another eastward view along West Chester Pike of the Ridley Creek Bridge and the Garrett Farm property. This c. 1900 photograph was taken from a point further west than the previous one. A park area straddles the western side of the Garrett Farm property today. (Chester County Historical Society, West Chester, Pennsylvania.)

This May 1899 Gilbert Cope photograph looks south from Dutton Mill Road toward West Chester Pike and shows an open-air trolley car traveling along the road. The building to the right is the former Willistown Inn and Post Office. Today, it houses a financial services office. The building on the left also stands today and is the site of a glass and mirror business. (Chester County Historical Society, West Chester, Pennsylvania.)

Here is another view of the former Willistown Inn and Post Office from the 1950s. This view looks east along West Chester Pike. (Chester County Historical Society, West Chester, Pennsylvania.)

This view, also from the 1950s, is of the former Willistown Inn and Post Office building and looks southwest along West Chester Pike. (Chester County Historical Society, West Chester, Pennsylvania.)

Pictured is the Jacob Smedley Homestead, which dates to 1766. It stood on the south side of West Chester Pike in the Willistown Knoll section of the township. Today, some of these buildings have been incorporated into the design of the Willistown Woods residential property at Stoneham Drive. This photograph was taken in December 1899. Quaker George Smedley came to the United States from Derbyshire, England, in 1683 and purchased land from William Penn. Some of his descendants settled in Willistown. (Chester County Historical Society, West Chester, Pennsylvania.)

Eight

WESTTOWN TOWNSHIP

Westtown Township was established in 1685, and its first settlers were English Quakers. In 1810, the population was 790 residents. In 2010, the population was 10,827. West Chester Pike passes through Westtown Township rather quickly, a distance of about one mile.

The township line begins just west of Hunter's Run Boulevard near the Kirkwood Fitness & Raquetball Clubs and ends at Manley Road. (Eric Hartline.)

The farm of Gertrude Riley McDaniel, seen in this 1941 photograph, was located on the southwest corner of West Chester Pike and Chester Road (Route 352) in Westtown. Most of the land pictured here is now part of the SS. Simon and Jude Catholic Church and School property. The parish was founded in May 1961, and the original church and school were built in 1962. A new church was built and opened in 2005. The house in the center of the photograph remains today. It has been expanded and serves as the church rectory and offices. (SS. Simon and Jude Catholic Church.)

Ground-breaking ceremonies for the soon-to-be-built SS. Simon and Jude Catholic Church and School are shown here in 1961. Presiding in the center of the photograph with a shovel in his hand is church pastor Fr. Joseph Cavanaugh. To his immediate left is Archbishop John Krol. (SS. Simon and Jude Catholic Church.)

Students and teachers line up for a dedication ceremony outside the new SS. Simon and Jude Catholic School in this September 1962 photograph. At the far right is church pastor Fr. Joseph Cavanaugh. In the background is the sign for the Esso gas station, which stood at West Chester Pike and Chester Road. Esso later became Exxon. (SS. Simon and Jude Catholic Church.)

An aerial view of McLaughlin's Exxon station on the northwest corner of West Chester Pike and Chester Road (Route 352) is seen in this mid-1970s photograph. Owner John McLaughlin operated the station at this location from 1971 to 2006. The station site is now occupied by a recycling business that opened in 2012. Behind the station was a Wawa food market, which closed in 2011. A new, larger Wawa food market and gas station has opened just west of this location. Next to the Wawa is a bank branch office. That site remains a bank office today. (John McLaughlin.)

Nine

EAST GOSHEN TOWNSHIP

East Goshen Township was originally part of a 5,000-acre parcel of land known as the Welsh Tract, which was purchased from William Penn in 1681. The Welsh Quakers who settled in the area named their village Goshenville, derived from the biblical name "Goshen," or "promised land." Goshen Township was established in 1704 and encompassed present-day West Chester Borough, East Goshen, and West Goshen Townships as well as part of Westtown Township. East Goshen was established in 1817.

West Chester Pike crosses the eastern boundary of East Goshen Township at Manley Road. It crosses its western boundary at Ellis Lane. (Eric Hartline.)

This c. 1950 photograph looks west along West Chester Pike toward the Milltown section of the township. The exact location is unknown. It appears to be between Manley Road and Westtown Way. (East Goshen Township.)

This undated photograph is of the William Chalfont House, which stood along the south side of West Chester Pike near Chester Hollow Road. It was torn down in the late 1960s, when the Summit House Condominiums were built. (East Goshen Township.)

This early 1930s photograph of children riding bikes and sledding was taken on Locust Street just south of West Chester Pike near Westtown Way in the Goshen Heights section of the township. (East Goshen Township.)

This photograph provides a westward view along West Chester Pike at Westtown Way. It was taken on June 3, 1954, the last day for regular trolley service along West Chester Pike. An eastbound trolley has just gone past the West Chester Water Works facility and a Philadelphia Suburban Transportation Co. substation in the Milltown section of East Goshen at Chester Creek. A sign on the right indicates a left turn to the Westtown School. (Bob Quay Sr.)

This 1899 view looks northwest along West Chester Pike from Westtown Way. The tall smoke stack on the left is part of the West Chester Pumping Station near Chester Creek. The Chester Creek Bridge span can also be seen. The buildings on the right (at the intersection with Reservoir Road) are the Sheaf of Wheat Inn and a stone barn. (Chester County Historical Society, West Chester, Pennsylvania.)

This is a c. 1890 view of the West Chester Pumping Station and the Sheaf of Wheat Inn from Westtown Way. The large barn in the center of the photograph is part of the William Hoopes Farm property. The row of buildings to the left is the Milltown section of the township. (East Goshen Township.)

Here is a close-up view of the Sheaf of Wheat Inn on the northwest corner of West Chester Pike and Reservoir Road. Built around 1720, it is seen in a Gilbert Cope photograph from 1899. The inn was a gathering place for locals and a popular stopping point for travelers on their way to and from Philadelphia. (Chester County Historical Society, West Chester, Pennsylvania.)

Here is another view of the Sheaf of Wheat Inn looking northeast from West Chester Pike in 1899. Three men are gathered on the front porch, while a horse carriage from the Rose Hill Farm sits in the dirt driveway. Trolley tracks can be seen on the far right corner of the photograph. The building still stands today and is used as office space. (East Goshen Township.)

This c. 1900 view looks east along West Chester Pike from a vantage point just west of the Sheaf of Wheat Inn (left). The trolley tracks for the Philadelphia–to–West Chester line can be seen at right, running along the south side of the pike. This view looks from the Milltown section of the township toward the Goshen Heights section. (Hagley Museum and Library.)

The home of George Ashbridge III sat behind the Sheaf of Wheat Inn at the intersection with Reservoir Road. It was built around 1760. Ashbridge operated a gristmill on the south side of West Chester Pike. This May 1899 photograph was taken by Gilbert Cope. The house still stands today and is used as an office building. (Chester County Historical Society, West Chester, Pennsylvania.)

This Gilbert Cope photograph from 1899 looks east along West Chester Pike toward the Sheaf of Wheat Inn (left) as a trolley makes it way along the pike. Trolley service from Philadelphia to West Chester via the pike started in 1899 and continued until 1954. (Chester County Historical Society, West Chester, Pennsylvania.)

In this eastward view, two boys stand in the middle of West Chester Pike at the top of the hill located just west of Reservoir Road. The front porch of the Sheaf of Wheat Inn can be seen to the left in the distance. The boys are probably standing near where Bob Wagner's Flooring America stands today, close to Valley Drive. (Hagley Museum and Library.)

Pictured here is a building that was known locally as the c. 1750 Toll House. The stone house stood on the south side of West Chester Pike near present-day Valley Drive. It was demolished in 1989 to make way for the construction of Bob Wagner's Flooring America. (East Goshen Township.)

This large stone barn was part of the William Hoopes Farm property. It was built in 1870 on the north side of West Chester Pike just west of Reservoir Road. The barn was demolished in 1986. (East Goshen Township.)

This 1920s photograph was taken at a Blue Sunoco gas station and automobile repair business on West Chester Pike in the Milltown section of the township. The station was owned and operated by George Entriken, according to an advertisement that accompanied this photograph. (East Goshen Township.)

Seen here is the Thomas C. Supplee Farm Market, which sat on the north side of West Chester Pike near Ellis Lane. This photograph was taken in the 1950s. A Firestone Tires outlet operates on this site today. (East Goshen Township.)

This is a 1963 aerial view of West Chester Pike near Ellis Lane, which is just out of view to the right. This view looks southwest along the pike from above the Goshen Fire Company property on Park Avenue. Open fields characterize the south side of West Chester Pike at this time and location. The road in the center of the photograph leading from West Chester Pike is an emergency access road to the Goshen Fire Company property. It remains there today. (East Goshen Township.)

The Goshen Fire Company building on Park Avenue (north of West Chester Pike near Ellis Lane) is seen in a 1967 photograph. The building has been expanded several times over the years. (East Goshen Township.)

This 1952 photograph from the Goshen Fair features the judging of livestock, which was a highlight of the fair. Here, Black Angus cattle are being judged. In the 1950s, East Goshen was still a largely rural farming community. While the township's landscape has since changed from rural to suburban, the Goshen Fair is still held each year on the Goshen Fire Company property at West Chester Pike and Ellis Lane and still features livestock as well as music, games, and amusements. (East Goshen Township.)

Ten

WEST GOSHEN
TOWNSHIP AND
WEST CHESTER BOROUGH

As previously mentioned, present-day West Goshen Township grew out of Goshen Township. It was established in 1817 and started primarily as a farming community. Soon, however, it was home to a number of different businesses and trades. At the time of the 1820 census, the township population was 757. In the 1900s, the township began to transform from a farming community into a suburban community. The 1960s and 1970s were decades of great growth and development. Today, the population is more than 20,000.

Moving from east to west, West Chester Pike enters West Goshen at Ellis Road. West Chester Pike ends when it merges with Paoli Pike near the West Chester Borough line. The township's western border with Route 3 is near Bolmar Street. (Eric Hartline.)

The Goshen Baptist Church is shown here around 1899 at its original location on West Chester Pike and East Strasburg Road in what is now West Goshen Township. This church was built in 1874 to replace a previous church, which was built in 1809 and destroyed by fire. (Hagley Museum and Library.)

This c. 1900 photograph of the Goshen Baptist Church shows an eastward view at West Chester Pike and East Strasburg Road. Trolley tracks can be seen on the right. The church remained at this location until 1970, when the current church was built farther east on West Chester Pike between Chester Hollow and Waterview Roads in what is now East Goshen Township. When the new church was built in 1970, the graves from the old church cemetery were carefully disinterred and, along with the gravestones, moved to the current site. (Hagley Museum and Library.)

This 1953 photograph looks south from West Chester Pike just east of Route 202 (the West Chester Bypass) in the Chatwood section of West Goshen. Pictured is the entranceway to an inn on the old Charles H. Sheller farm property. From the 1920s to the 1930s, this property was the site of the Chester County Fair Grounds, where horse shows and auto races were held. Today, this is the entrance to Rolling Green Memorial Park, a cemetery property. It is beside a Chevrolet automobile dealership. (Chester County Historical Society, West Chester, Pennsylvania.)

This photograph was taken on June 6, 1954, at the intersection of West Chester Pike and Route 202 (the West Chester Bypass). This view looks eastward just west of the bypass. This was during a special run of the trolley dubbed the "Last Run," when regular service along the trolley line was being ended. The trolley operators are unidentified. Many people rode the trolley that day to be part of this historic occasion. (Greco family.)

This image from the Ned Goode Collection was taken in July 1960 and looks west on West Chester Pike just east of Prospect Avenue, shortly before entering West Chester. At right is the driveway for the Virginia A. Love Nursery School and Kindergarten at 835 West Chester Pike. Today, the buildings on this block are private residences or commercial offices. (Chester County Historical Society, West Chester, Pennsylvania.)

This image is also from the Ned Goode Collection and dates to July 1960. It looks east on West Chester Pike near Prospect Avenue. In the distance, the overpass for Route 202 (the West Chester Bypass) can be seen. An automobile is heading west toward West Chester. It has just passed a sign on the right that reads "Groceries" and "Ice Cream." By the time of this photograph, the trolley tracks had been taken up, but the roadway had not yet been widened to four lanes. (Chester County Historical Society, West Chester, Pennsylvania.)

West Chester Borough grew out of the sleepy crossroads village of Turk's Head in the 1700s. Originally, it was part of Goshen Township, which also included present-day East Goshen and West Goshen Townships, and part of Westtown Township. It became the county seat of Chester County in 1786. It was incorporated as a borough in 1799. West Chester Pike/Pennsylvania Route 3 ends at West Chester. Here, it merges with Paoli Pike and continues one-way west as Gay Street. The route departs West Chester eastbound by Market Street. After West Chester, the route splits into Pennsylvania Route 162 (Strasburg Road) and US Route 322 (Downingtown Pike). Both roads continue westward through Chester County toward Lancaster County. (Eric Hartline.)

This c. 1920 photograph shows a street sign welcoming visitors to West Chester. A trolley can be seen in the distance making its way down the road. At this point, Route 3/West Chester Pike has become East Gay Street in West Chester. This sign stood along the road in proximity to Penn Street and Adams Street near where the West Chester Recreation Department Building stands today. The fence to the right belongs to the old Sharples Baseball Field. (Chester County Historical Society, West Chester, Pennsylvania.)

This trolley is westbound on a snowy Gay Street near the intersection with Matlack Street. It is approaching the center of town and the end of the trolley line. This photograph was taken on March 1, 1941. (David H. Cope.)

This c. 1920 photograph shows a Philadelphia and West Chester Traction Company trolley. (Chester County Historical Society, West Chester, Pennsylvania.)

This image shows the last regularly scheduled trolley car run from Sixty-ninth Street in Upper Darby to West Chester on June 4, 1954. Here, the trolley has reached the end of the line at Gay and High Streets and is on its way out of town, bound for Sixty-ninth Street. The car was quite full that day, as one can see. (Chester County Historical Society, West Chester, Pennsylvania.)

This trolley car has reached the end of the line: Gay and High Streets in West Chester. This photograph was taken on August 8, 1925. This view looks west on Gay Street from the north side of the road. (Stanley F. Bowman Jr.)

Here is a c. 1940 photograph of the Shortline/Red Arrow Bus Lines Station at High and Gay Streets in West Chester. This view looks from the southwest corner of the intersection toward the northeast corner. Today, the ground floor of this apartment building is home to a Rite Aid Pharmacy. Across the street is an Iron Hill Brewery and Restaurant. (Chester County Historical Society, West Chester, Pennsylvania.)

This 1950s photograph was taken near the end of the trolley line at Gay and High Streets. This view looks east along Gay Street. The building behind the trolley (at right) is the former Vincent's Restaurant. It is now called the Side Bar and Restaurant. (Chester County Historical Society, West Chester, Pennsylvania.)

BIBLIOGRAPHY

Ashmead, Henry Graham. *History of Delaware County, Pennsylvania*. Philadelphia: L.H. Everts & Co., 1884 (reprint 2010).

Chester County Historical Society with the Chester County Camera Club. *Chester County*. Charleston, SC: Arcadia Publishing, 2004.

DeGraw, Ronald. *The Red Arrow: A History of One of the Most Successful Suburban Transit Companies in the World*. Haverford, PA: Haverford Press, 1972.

————. *Red Arrow: The First Hundred Years, 1848–1948*. Glendale, CA: Interurban Press, 1985.

DiFilippo, Thomas J. *The History and Development of Upper Darby Township*. 2nd ed. Upper Darby, PA: Upper Darby Historical Society, 1992.

Driscoll, Christopher, and Janice Elston. *Newtown Square*. Charleston, SC: Arcadia Publishing, 2009.

Faris, John T. *Old Roads Out of Philadelphia*. Philadelphia: Washington Square Press, J.B. Lippincott Co., 1917.

Gordon, Linda M. *East Goshen Township*. Charleston, SC: Arcadia Publishing, 2009.

Haverford Township Historical Society. *Haverford Township*. Charleston, SC: Arcadia Publishing, 2003.

Mathis, Mike. *Marple and Newtown Townships*. Charleston, SC: Arcadia Publishing, 1998.

Mowday, Bruce Edward. *West Chester*. Charleston, SC: Arcadia Publishing, 2005.

Rorer, Beverly, and Barbara Marinelli for the Upper Darby Historical Society. *Upper Darby*. Charleston, SC: Arcadia Publishing, 2011.

DISCOVER THOUSANDS OF LOCAL HISTORY BOOKS
FEATURING MILLIONS OF VINTAGE IMAGES

Arcadia Publishing, the leading local history publisher in the United States, is committed to making history accessible and meaningful through publishing books that celebrate and preserve the heritage of America's people and places.

Find more books like this at
www.arcadiapublishing.com

Search for your hometown history, your old stomping grounds, and even your favorite sports team.

Consistent with our mission to preserve history on a local level, this book was printed in South Carolina on American-made paper and manufactured entirely in the United States. Products carrying the accredited Forest Stewardship Council (FSC) label are printed on 100 percent FSC-certified paper.

MADE IN THE USA